How to make Cookies

Paul Humphrey

Photography by Chris Fairclough

W
FRANKLIN WATTS
LONDON • SYDNEY

First published in 2006 by
Franklin Watts
338 Euston Road
London NW1 3BH

Franklin Watts Australia
Hachette Children's Books
Level 17/207 Kent Street
Sydney NSW 2000

© 2006 Franklin Watts

ISBN: 0 7496 6608 0 (hbk)
ISBN: 0 7496 6859 8 (pbk)

Dewey classification number: 641.8'654

A CIP catalogue record for this book is available
from the British Library.

Planning and production by Discovery Books Limited
Editor: Rachel Tisdale
Designer: Ian Winton
Photography: Chris Fairclough
Series advisors: Diana Bentley MA and Dee Reid MA,
Fellows of Oxford Brookes University

The author, packager and publisher would like to thank the following
people for their participation in this book: Jack Moran and Lucas Tisdale.

Printed in China

Contents

What you need

Do you like cookies?
Here's how to make
star cookies.

These are the
things you
will need:

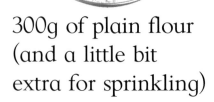

300g of plain flour
(and a little bit
extra for sprinkling)

150g of
caster
sugar

1 large
egg

2 teaspoons of
vanilla essence

250g
of soft butter

A fork

4

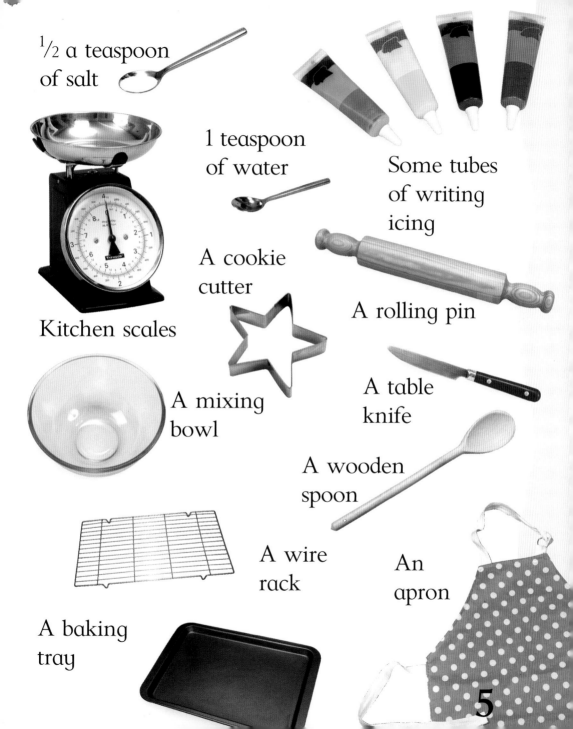

$^1/_2$ a teaspoon
of salt

1 teaspoon
of water

Some tubes
of writing
icing

Kitchen scales

A cookie
cutter

A rolling pin

A mixing
bowl

A table
knife

A wooden
spoon

A wire
rack

An
apron

A baking
tray

Getting ready

Wash your hands carefully.

Ask an adult to set the oven to 180°C (gas mark 4).

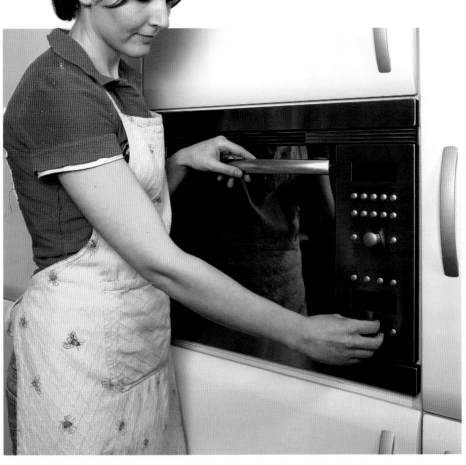

Measuring the ingredients

Use the kitchen scales to measure out the flour, butter and sugar.

Keep the
ingredients
separate.

Cut the butter into
small pieces.

Beating the ingredients

Beat the butter and sugar together in a bowl.

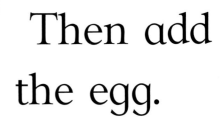

Then add the egg.

Now add the vanilla essence.

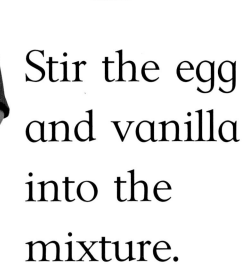

Stir the egg and vanilla into the mixture.

Adding the salt and flour

Add the salt. Then add the flour a little at a time.

Stir the mixture.

Keep stirring and adding
the flour until you get a
smooth dough.

Rolling out the dough

Sprinkle some flour onto your worktop.

Rub some onto the rolling pin.

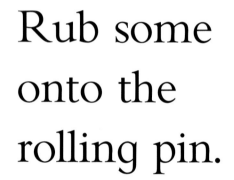

Now roll out the
dough until it is
about 5mm thick.

Cutting the cookies

Cut out the cookies
with the cookie cutter.
Cut them close together
so that you can make
lots of cookies.

Squash together the leftover dough. Roll it out again and cut out more cookies.

Baking the cookies

Lay the cookies onto the baking tray.

Ask an adult to put them in the oven.

18

The cookies will take 12 minutes to bake.

Cooling the cookies

When they are cooked ask an adult to take them out of the oven.

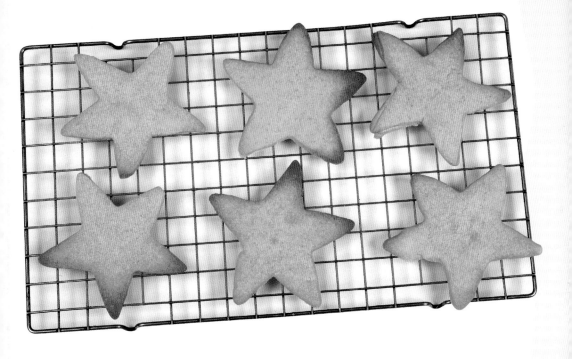

Put them on a
wire rack to cool.

Decorating the cookies

Decorate your cookies using the tubes of writing icing.

Finally, share
your cookies with
your friends.

Steps

Can you remember all of the steps to make your cookies?

1. Wash your hands.

2. Set the oven to 180°C.

3. Measure the ingredients.

4. Cut up the butter.

5. Beat the butter, sugar, egg and vanilla essence.

6. Add the salt and flour to make dough.

7. Roll the dough and cut cookies.

8. Bake the cookies.

9. Decorate and eat your cookies.